T. N. T.

IT ROCKS THE EARTH

A philosophy for today, tomorrow and thereafter with some practical suggestions as to how to get what you want in life.

By CLAUDE M. BRISTOL
Writer and Lecturer
(formerly Vice-President of a well-known Pacific Coast Investment Banking firm)

T. N. T.

Martino Fine Books
Eastford, CT
2017

Martino Fine Books
P.O. Box 913,
Eastford, CT 06242 USA

ISBN 978-1-68422-126-4

Copyright 2017
Martino Fine Books

All rights reserved. No new contribution to this publication may be reproduced, stored in a retrieval system, or transmitted, in any form or by any means, electronic, mechanical, photocopying, recording, or otherwise, without the prior permission of the Publisher.

Cover Design Tiziana Matarazzo

Printed in the United States of America On 100% Acid-Free Paper

T. N. T.
IT ROCKS THE EARTH

A philosophy for today, tomorrow and thereafter with some practical suggestions as to how to get what you want in life.

By CLAUDE M. BRISTOL
Writer and Lecturer
(formerly Vice-President of a well-known Pacific Coast Investment Banking firm)

T. N. T.

Published by
T. N. T.—DISTRIBUTORS
3204 East Burnside Street
PORTLAND, OREGON

Copyright 1932
Copyright 1933
(*Revised Edition*)
by
CLAUDE M. BRISTOL
All rights reserved

No part of this is to be used without the permission of the author.

First Edition—January 1932
Second Edition—July 1932
Third Edition—March 1933
Fourth Edition—October 1933

To
R. C. W.
who located T. N. T. in my pocket

To
M. J. E.
who caused me to find it

To
L. B. E.
who had me use it

To
E. L. B.
who added to it

AND TO

all others who aided me in assembling my supply of T. N. T., this high explosive is affectionately dedicated.

FOR EVERY EXECUTIVE and SALESMAN

"This book should be in the hands of every executive and salesman, and studied at regular intervals. When followed, it will bring happiness and success to anyone."—HORACE MECKLEM, well known member, *National Association of Life Underwriters*.

FOREWORD

It was that period approaching the end of the second year of the great economic depression when hopefulness had almost vanished from business life, and everyone was overwhelmed with fear, that Mr. Claude M. Bristol, my close business associate of many years standing, astounded me by relating a most amazing experience in having found "THAT SOMETHING" for which he had been searching many years.

As he revealed the truths which had come to him I, at first, was skeptical, but as he took me along with him, I, too, began to see the light which only stimulated my ambition for further knowledge of the theme of how to live powerfully by adopting that science which relates to the development of the human personality.

I realize that there was a great change for good coming over myself, and sensed the possibilities of what could be done if the members of our own organization put the author's teachings into practice, and forthwith arrangements were made for him to talk to our entire staff. The immediate reponse of every member of our organization in demanding a copy—followed by the most remark-

T. N. T.

able transformation of individuals and organization, brought home the positive conviction to me that the message contained in his theme was exactly what the world most needed, and that a great service could be rendered by publishing same for general distribution.

In "*T.N.T.—It Rocks the Earth*," you are told exactly how to acquire a wonderful secret, that **POWER**, or whatever you wish to call it, which, when accepted and developed through a process of right thinking, creates a philosophy of life which sweeps away all obstacles and brings that which every human desires: success, happiness and contentment.

If it were not for the fact that I am intimately acquainted with the author I would pause to wonder where he acquired those facts and principles which he sets forth in his story, but suffice to say that I know that he knows what he is talking about, and he clearly outlines a system of mechanics which can be used by every one—irrespective of his or her walk in life.

Do exactly as he says, put his plan into operation—and I also promise you that almost over night you will be transformed and the things for which you have wished all your life will be yours. Your fears, trials and tribulations will fade into the mists. The door of yesterday will be closed forever. A grand and glorious feeling will engulf you and you will smile, and when you do, the world will smile with you.

I know it. I believe it and it is so.

FRANK W. CAMP.

— *Tap* — *Tap* — *Tap* —

"My statement that the book has done more to stimulate business here during the past year than any other single factor or agency is based upon statements to me by numerous executives who have been using the theme successfully in their business. Any who reads it three or four times understandingly will easily appreciate why it makes for more business and profits."

ROBERT M. MOUNT, *Manager*
PORTLAND BETTER BUSINESS BUREAU, INC.

— *Tap* — *Tap* — *Tap* —

Note to fourth and subsequent editions.

POTENTIALLY EVERY MAN IS A KING—EVERY WOMAN A QUEEN!!

"Everyone of normal intelligence has the desire to accomplish great things but does not force the stored-up ability locked up within himself to assert its full power. Your booklet surely is the master key to the lock and should inspire its readers to a realization of such desires."
                                        JOHN D. CURTIS, Boston, Mass.

A mere scanning of this book will do you little, if any good. It must be studied and reflected upon, and the principles set forth conscientiously and sincerely applied. It has worked wonders for thousands of people and it will do the same for you when you accept the theme with an open mind, and follow the tenets set forth herein and **BELIEVE** whole-heartedly.

Thomas M. Roche, New York City, associate director of one of the largest firms of business counselors and sales directors in the world, and an enthusiast of the book, said:
> *"It isn't something you can skim through and throw aside. Each page needs rereading many times to get even a part of it."*

Therefore, do not loan or give this book away. Make it your companion—referring to it daily. When you understand and thoughtfully apply the whole theme, "MIRACLES" will be performed.

REREAD IT   REREAD IT   REREAD IT

DETONATING CAPS

"He who does not know what the world is, does not know where he is. And he who does not know for what purpose the world exists, does not know who he is, nor what the world is."

A First Century Message

— *Tap* — *Tap* — *Tap* —

For those of you who seek to learn and make progress, I gently lay this in your laps. I do so without the slightest fear but that it will turn your world entirely upside down—bringing you health, wealth, success and happiness, providing you understand and accept.

Remember T.N.T. is a dangerously high explosive so when you gather it closely, handle it gently.

Do Not Misuse It Down through the centuries its power has destroyed those who sought to misuse it, therefore **exercise great care** that it is used only for good.

T. N. T.

It can be proved by the teachings of the Bible, certain well established laws of physics, and last but not least, just plain common sense. Read and determine for yourself whether or not the proofs I offer stand by themselves.

Some of you may see only the spiritual side, others recognize the scientific truths, and still others may accept it as just a practical operating device to put you on the road to success. No matter—many know the truth and for you who will open your minds the light will pour in with dazzling white brilliancy.

I'm indebted to an old friend of mine, an expert on X-Ray, and electrical high frequency apparatus, who, when I was a boy experimenting with electricity, called to my attention the first bit of powerful T.N.T. in my pocket. Then I didn't know what it was and didn't understand, but fortunately it has remained there all through the years. As I look back I realize why he didn't **Make** me understand what it was. He believed in me and knew that when I was ready to accept it I would. It's taken nearly 30 years, during which time I sought up and down the highways, looking, seeking and searching for the **SECRET—T.N.T.**

Feel in Your Pocket

All of the time there was some in my pocket—mine for the mere reaching. However, I've got a firm grip on it now and I will divide it graciously, knowing if used wisely it will blow away all obstacles and straighten out the road on which you've been wanting to travel all your life.

For many years I was a newspaper man and frequently I was behind the scenes. I met great men and women, interviewed famous people. Naturally I studied them and tried to understand what peculiar qualities they possessed that placed them above the others, but their secret evaded me.

Then came the war and I wondered why others made progress while I seemed to be *"blocked"* in my own ambitions. The war did teach me, however, that I could sleep in the mud, eat moldy bread and live to laugh about it. This is part of my T.N.T. so remember what I learned. It helped me to give old man **FEAR** a solar plexus blow and I believe it will help you.

Hoping to find a royal road to fortune I read hundreds of the so-called "**Success**" books and they took me nowhere. I did the same with books on philosophy, psychology and still the

.T.N.T

great **Secret** kept just a jump ahead of me. I joined secret fraternal organizations, hoping that I might find that which I sought. However, just like the bit of T.N.T. in my pocket the **Secret** was in every book, in the great orders, everywhere, and in fact, right under my very nose but something kept me from it. You will have to determine for yourself what keeps you from it if you don't get it from T.N.T. It's there—if you don't find it in the printed word look between the lines—as I've done my best to present it to you.

Following the war I became a member of a coast-wide investment banking organization and during **Are You Afraid?** the years I cherished quite a dream— as did thousands of others in all lines of business—only to discover that the air castles which I builded were on an unstable foundation. That something which turned the world upside down financially entirely obliterated my air castles, and I became **Afraid**. I got lost in the fog. Everywhere I turned something fell in on me.

As an executive of the organization my responsibilities multiplied. Our business, due to the economic changes which were taking place in the world, faced a crisis, and many people failing to understand the catastrophe which had overtaken business everywhere were critical. All of which brought worry and many sleepless nights. I found myself dreading to go to my work—fearing that each day would bring added misery.

The weeks went on and conditions got worse and worse. I was baffled. Several times I talked about getting out of the business and one day in the latter part of June, 1931, I made up my mind to leave. I mentioned it to one of the women with whom I had been associated for several years and saw nothing but reproach in her eyes.

That night I tried to sleep. Again I found it impossible. I paced the floor for hours—when at about 3:30 in the morning I suddenly stopped and sat down. I was face to face with myself. I could follow the inclination to run and leave the others to carry on by themselves, or I could stay and do my share; a duty which I knew was mine. I caught myself saying almost aloud: "*Right is right. It's always been right. It can't be otherwise;*" something I had been taught since infancy.

Suddenly there appeared to be an unfoldment.

T.N.T.

Out of the air came a voice saying: "*What have*
Out *you been seeking all these years? What were*
of the *you taught? What did you learn? Where*
Air *have you been? Where are you going?*" I
jumped to my feet crying: "*I know it. I've got it
now. It's the secret. That's what they tried to teach
you. It is the* **Royal Secret**, *too.*"

Something told me that I would find those identical words in a book which had many years before been given me and which I had tried to read, failed to understand and put aside. It was written by a great man, Albert Pike, a mystic, a poet and a scholar. Grabbing it from the shelf —feverishly I ran through the pages. The words were there and I understood immediately.

I now had the key. I could see a broad smooth highway and at the end of that highway a perfect flood of gorgeously beautiful
Open radiance. "*That's the road you are on now.*
Your *What a simpleton you have been! They tried*
Mind *to teach you, they tried to help you and you
kept your mind closed—thinking that you alone could
find the road and stay on it.*"

I was nearly overcome with the sheer joy of it all. My fears, my worries had disappeared. I

(10)

smiled. I knew that I was right and that everything would be right for me from then on. I slept like a baby.

There was a different atmosphere in the office that day. The oppressive black clouds which hung over us began to fade away. I told the woman—she with the reproachful eyes—what had happened, and she smiled a knowing smile. She helped me get back on the track and I can never repay her.

As one learned man said: "*All of us are born with the ability to differentiate between right and wrong, and with the ability to achieve, but some of us must run head-on into a stone wall, smash ourselves to bits before we really know what it's all about.*" I hit the wall with a terrific crash and it was the greatest and finest thing that ever happened to me.

Many noting the transformation asked for an explanation. I told some of my closest friends. Knowing it will help I give it to all of you.

— Tap — Tap — Tap —

— Tap — Tap — Tap —

T. N. T.

Since I caught this theme the book has been put to use by thousands of individuals, firms and organizations. In addition I have talked and lectured, in person and over the radio, to many additional thousands and I am very happy to say that, without exception, phenomenal results have been obtained by those who have understood and applied the principles and mechanics outlined herein.

— Tap — Tap — Tap —

— Tap — Tap — Tap —

The morale of our whole organization was at its lowest ebb. Everyone was discouraged. **Afraid.** By the very necessity of things we had to do an about-face.

My job was doing everything I could to help the other fellow because I knew it was right. At first I was perplexed as to the methods I should employ to help them, but I used my own system in calling upon the subconscious, and the inner voice said that I should talk to them.

Right Is Right

Some were skeptical, but I said to myself: "*I can prove that I am right,*" and during the week that followed I spent every waking hour reviewing the books that I had studied through the years. Naturally the Bible came first; then followed studies in Yogiism, the philosophies of the old Greek and Roman masters and of the later day teachers and students. I again deliberated over the Meditations of Marcus Aurelius Antoninus. Reread Hudson's Law of Psychic Phenomena, another book, "*The Gist of It,*" written by a brilliant physician, Haydon Rochester. Again I studied my books on physics, electricity and those on the vibrations of light and discovered that not only was I right, as I knew I would be, but that peculiarly the same general basic principles ran through them all. I reread numerous books on psychology and found the same story everywhere. Subsequently I quoted excerpts, and lo and behold, things began to move.

— Tap — Tap — Tap —

It has occurred to me again and again that all men and women who use this **POWER** are showmen, or to use the words of my newspaper days,

T. N. T.

headliners—those who hit the front page. Something causes them to toss away the bushel basket under which they hide their heads and they arise above the commonplace.

Where Is Your Niche?

Surely you will agree they may have the **POWER** to the Nth degree, but if they do not become headliners they never get a niche in the hall of fame. It doesn't follow that they are newspaper publicity seekers, because some of them are very reticent—and by their very reticence are showmen. Others adopt certain peculiarities or use certain devices to make them stand out from their fellowmen. Some wear an efficacious smile, others scowl—and still others have a certain charm of manner. Long hair, whiskers and sideburns play their part. Flowing robes and distinctive dress are worn by others. The showmanship of some is evidenced by red neckties, others by spats, affected manners.

Many master the art of oratory, the science of warfare, banking, statesmanship, politics, the arts—but all of them stand out in the full glare of the calcium—headliners.

The number is legion. I mention a few of those

of history and today: Desmosthenes, Nero, Julius Caesar, Christopher Columbus, Cleopatra, Balzac, de Maupassant, Sir Isaac Newton, Joan of Arc, Cromwell, Edgar Allen Poe, Benjamin Franklin, Alexander Hamilton, Bismark, Graham Bell, General Grant, Cecil Rhodes, P. T. Barnum, Clemenceau, Kitchener, Woodrow Wilson, Joffre, Sir Thomas Lipton, Foch, Mussolini, Winston Churchill, Charles E. Hughes, Lloyd George, Mahatma Gandhi, Ramsey MacDonald, Will Rogers, Douglas Fairbanks, Roosevelt, Henry Ford, Lindbergh, Alfred E. Smith, Lenin and Hitler. They have been and are found in every walk of life.

Gandhi uses this **POWER**, I am sure, and I think he is the greatest headliner of present times. You can find many pictures showing him in the modern civilized garb of man, but today, and for several years he has kept his hair cropped short, worn a loin cloth and a pair of huge spectacles. I have no right to say that. Gandhi affected this attire for any particular purpose, but I believe he has done it to focus the world's attention upon himself for India's cause.

I make no attempt to explain why those who use

T. N. T.

this **POWER** are showmen. You'll have to determine that for yourself. But remember—

> *"A city that is set upon a hill cannot be hid. Neither do men light a candle and place it under a bushel . . ."*

Again—

> *"The great truths of life become known only to those who are prepared to accept them."*

I repeat. Thousands who used the **POWER** for evil brought on their own destruction. We get out of life exactly what we put into it—no more, no less. When we put in good thoughts, constructive efforts and do good then we receive like in return, for—

> *"Whatsoever a man soweth, that shall he also reap."*

Detonating Caps are now set! Caution signals are out. **Be Careful!**

"A man's true greatness lies in the consciousness of an honest purpose in life, founded on a just estimate of himself and everything else, on frequent self-examinations, and a steady obedience to the rule which he knows to be right, without troubling himself about what others may think or say, or whether they do or do not do that which he thinks and says and does." MARCUS AURELIUS ANTONINUS.

— *Tap* — *Tap* — *Tap* —

There are thousands, yes, millions of people seeking the **SECRET**—the key to health, riches, happiness, contentment and a solution of their problems.

Through the ages many men and women had the **SECRET**, used the **POWER**, and I am positive you can acquire it too if you'll think as you

T. N. T.

read, accept and apply the ideas contained herein.

? What do you want?
Where are you going?

— *Tap* — *Tap* — *Tap* —

I repeat an old story:

Down on a levee in Mississippi, two niggers were dozing—one of them yawned, stretched his arms and sighed:

An Old, Old Story

"Gee, I wish I had a million watermelons."

The other nigger asked:

"Rastus, if you had a million watermelons, would you give me half of them?"

"No, sir!"

"Would you give me a quarter of them?"

"No, I wouldn't give you a quarter of them."

"Rastus, if you had a million watermelons wouldn't you give me even ten of them?"

"No, sir! I wouldn't give you ten of them."

"Well, wouldn't you give me one lousy watermelon?"

"Say, Sam, I wouldn't give you even a bite of one if I had a million watermelons."

"Why not, Rastus?"

"Because you're too lazy to wish for yourself."

There's much to be gleaned from that story. You'll understand as I proceed.

I am fully cognizant that some will scoff—there have always been scoffers, but scoffers never succeed. They never get any place in life — simply become envious, while the doer or the person who is moving forward has to jump over or go around them. They have nothing but a nuisance value in life. Some of you may dismiss all of this as you have done before—as you always will—but for those of you who are interested, are still willing to learn, I promise you can learn and make progress for yourself.

Scoffers Do Not Succeed

I take it there isn't an intelligent man or woman who isn't really interested in getting ahead, but I have often wondered if there isn't a negative quality in most of us which precludes us from really starting.

There's a saying I thoroughly believe in: "*If you*

T. N. T.

If You Believe It— It's So

believe it, it's so." Simply a cryptic statement or digest of what I give you. All the great teachers, Buddha, Confucius, Mohammed, Jesus and many philosophers taught a great fundamental idea. It is found in all religions, cults, creeds and sects. Everywhere runs the same general theme—the gist of which in my words is—"If you believe it, it's so."

I quote from the Bible: *"As a man thinketh in his heart—so is he." "As a man thinketh in his heart—so is he"*—*if you believe it, it's so.* Note the similarity? Reduce the whole thing to one word—"FAITH." I have heard many, many people say the day of miracles is past, but never in my life have I heard a thinker, a student or a believer make such a declaration. Surely, the days of Aladdin and his lamp are gone—perhaps they never existed—so with the magic wand, the magic carpet, and all of those thing of fairy tale and legend.

When I refer to miracles, I mean those things which can be accomplished through **FAITH**.

Believe in Yourself

FAITH in your belief; **FAITH** in Yourself; **FAITH** in the persons with whom you are associated. **FAITH** in a **Power**. **FAITH** in "THAT SOMETHING" which controls the destinies of everyone—and, if you can get that **FAITH** and dissipate the negative side, nothing in this world can stop you from acquiring what you desire.

While this may sound facetious, you can have anything obtainable if you really want it.

All of us are prone to calculate and weigh things, permitting the negative side to creep to the fore, and our thoughts evidence themselves in such remarks as *"It can't be done;" "I'm afraid;" "What will happen if I do it?" "People won't understand;" "It isn't worth the effort;" "I haven't the time"* and similar verbal alibis. If you haven't expressed these thoughts to yourself, then others have to you, and, through the power of suggestion, you have accepted them as your own conclusions.

Why the Alibis?

This same message has been written and delivered thousands of times. It runs through the Bible; you find it in the great fraternal orders; it led the three wise men; the crusaders carried it; every outstanding character of history has used it; Moses, Alexander the Great, Napoleon, Shakespeare, Washington, Lincoln, Roosevelt, Wilson,

T. N. T.

Benjamin Franklin, Edison, Dr. Steinmetz, Barnum, and thousands of others had a grasp of "THAT SOMETHING."

The wise men of all ages, the *"medicine men,"* religious leaders, great teachers, the Maya priests, the Yogis, the *"healers,"* the *"miracle men"*—all of them knew this secret. Some worked it one way, some another.

The Wise Men Knew

They were just human beings. If they knew and could achieve, so can you.

Halt! Think! Ponder! What made Mussolini?

What is it that Aimee has? Gypsy Smith? Billy Sunday? **BELIEF, FAITH**—only that, and the ability of a staunch believer to pass it on to the other fellow. It's the very keynote of all great religions. All big things are started by one person, one believer. It makes no difference where they got the idea originally. All great inventions are the outgrowth of the whole scheme—**FAITH, FAITH—BELIEF** in yourself, your ideas. All super-salesmen know this—they use the **POWER** —that's why they are super-salesmen. Every community drive, every forward movement, everything worth while succeeds because some one person has **FAITH** and is able to pass it on and on and on. Think about that—then think about it some more, and think of it again. Meditate over it, and you'll realize that every word is true.

Many envy the man or woman getting ahead, who appears to be a financial success, a power, an influence. Did you ever seek the explanation? Everything that anyone has ever done constructively has been done from within himself.

Don't Envy: Do

Every one of us, if put on the right track, can accomplish what he or she is after by keeping before him or her my own expression: *"If you believe it, it's so,"* and adopting the old adage: *"Where there's a will there's a way."* In other words, get that will power—that **FAITH**—that **BELIEF** working every minute of the day—24 hours of the day—7 days a week—365 days a year. And I promise you if it's done you will leave people around you in the progress you make as rapidly as high frequency electrical discharges oscillate through the ether.

T.N.T.

T. N. T.

Pause and think for a moment. What is organized propaganda? Nothing more, nothing less than a well developed plan to make you believe. You saw it work in the war days and if you're wide awake to what is going on around you, you know that it's being worked in every line of human endeavor today—just as it was worked thousands of years ago and as it always works. If you're reading the newspaper, listening to the radio and will keep in mind my theme, you will realize that all these speeches of our leaders, our great executives coming to us with clock-like regularity are being given with a purpose—to make us believe. Those men know it works.

**Stop!
Think!
Meditate!**

Mahatma Gandhi upon arriving in England to seek a solution of India's problems said: *"I'm doing this because a voice within me speaks."*

The Voice Speaks

Gandhi referred to *"something"* from within. Call it a **POWER**, call it something supernatural, call it anything you wish. Some refer to it as the subjective mind. Others call it the subconscious mind. Some instinct. Some universal thought. Still others to the impulses coming from within as hunches. Divine messages. Spiritualists refer to it as a voice from beyond. No matter what it is, it gets results, and now I show you how to acquire it.

First, however, permit me to set the stage by calling attention to the effect of repetition or reiteration. For example, take a pneumatic chisel—you have seen one used in breaking up solid concrete or piercing holes through steel. It's the tap, tap, tap, tap of that chisel with a terrific force behind which causes disintegration of the particles and makes a dent or hole in the object on which it is used.

Tap No. 1

All of us have heard of the old torture system of dripping water on the forehead. Perhaps you are familiar with Kipling's *"Boots."* It's the tramp, tramp of boots, boots, that makes men mad. It's the constant never-ending repetition that penetrates.

You are familiar with the first part of the picture and how repetition works on material things, but some of you may not thoroughly understand the second part, but here, too, it's the repetition that ultimately makes its impression upon the human mind.

T. N. T.

The fundamental of advertising is its repetition, its appeal by reiteration—*"It floats;" "There's a reason;" "I'd walk a mile;" "They're kind to your throat."* A hundred others all impressed on your consciousness by constant repetition—tap, tap, tap. Through the science of repetition you learned to multiply. Everything you ever memorized was impressed upon your consciousness through repetition. You are constantly (tap, tap, tap) being reminded to re-affirm (more tap, tap) your **FAITH** in your religious belief. The same science —again and again. Repetition, reiteration. Tap, tap, tap.

[marginal note: Reaffirmation and Repetition]

The connection between the conscious and the subconscious or subjective mind is close. Every student of the subject knows what may be accomplished by definitely contacting the subconscious. When you get a definite detailed picture in your conscious mind by using this process of reiteration or repetition and make the subconscious mind click, you have at your command a **POWER** that astounds.

We hear much about the power of suggestion.

The Science of Suggestion

We know how easy it is to make a person ill by constantly suggesting to him that he doesn't look well, etc. It's the constant mental review of his crime that makes a lawbreaker confess. As a newspaper man I have been in on many *"third degree"* sessions. I have seen detectives and prosecutors corner a single individual and shoot questions at that individual until his face was bathed in perspiration. It is the deadly repetition, the reiteration, the tap, tap, tap, through the power of suggestion which brings confession.

Skilled prosecutors, clever defenders appeal to the emotions of jurors, never to the conscious reason. And how do they do it? Simply by a process of repeating and emphasizing time after time the points they wish to stress. They do it with usage of words and variations of argument. Behind all there is that tap, tap, tap, tap—tapping—the subconscious—making the jurors believe.

If you will keep this idea of repetition in mind you will understand why members of a certain race of people are so successful in business. When families are gathered together, the subject of conversation is business, business. They talk their

T. N. T.

problems over—they keep before them constantly the idea of making money and making progress and never for a moment are they permitted to forget. And they stick toether.

The idea there was born of necessity, just like a machine or an article is born of necessity. We are all familiar with the old adage, *"Necessity is the mother of invention"*—and it is true of all human impulses and endeavors. A drowning man grabs at a straw. A starving man at a crust of bread. The impulses come when you get up against it. You who have been there know what you had to rely on in times of acute pressure, and whether or not you heard a little voice from within.

There can be no gainsaying that once you have made up your mind to do a thing it will be done, but the trouble with most of us is that we sidestep, vacillate, and seldom make up our minds to what we want or determine clearly the road on which we wish to travel. All daydreams and wishes would become realities if we kept them constantly before us—put fear behind—shoved away all reservations, ifs, ands and buts. Again, a lot of us think we know what we want when, as a matter of fact, we don't. This sounds paradoxical but, if

Where Are You Going?

each of us knew what he wanted, he would get it, provided he had the will-power, the stamina, the dynamic force, the fight to go after it.

Therefore, the first thing to do is get that spirit of determination. That may be obtained by constantly saying to yourself—"*I will*," "*I will*," "*I will*" and "*I will*" and **BELIEVE** it. Then before you know it you will have developed a will-power which, coupled with these other things I am about to explain, will change your whole scheme of things and get **YOU** on the road to success. If you haven't the desire to improve your own individual position in life, then you had better stop reading right now and burn this. However, should you have the desire, you are on your way to make progress.

No matter whether you be a salesman, an executive, a mechanic, a writer or what, or whether **What Do You Want?** you are after money, love, improvement in social position, in the legal profession or medical profession, it makes absolutely no difference. You can utilize this **POWER** and acquire every single thing you want—whether it be a pair of shoes or a mansion.

T. N. T.

Now if you have the desire, the foundation is laid. Get a perfect detailed picture of the exact thing, or things, you wish. If it is increased sales, fix the exact amounts; if it's something you want the other fellow to do for you, the love of a woman or the love of a man, a new suit of clothes or a new automobile—anything and everything. No matter what you are after under this system you can have it, **provided the object of desire is morally right, and the picture definite and positive.**

Tap No. 2

> "*He who knows how to plant, shall not have his plant uprooted; He who knows how to hold a thing, shall not have it taken away.*"
> LAO TZŬ, THE CHINESE MYSTIC, 600 B.C.

When you have the picture firmly in mind begin using the tap, tap system as I have outlined. It is going to be the repetition, the reiteration of that picture upon the subconscious mind that will cause the little voice from within to speak and point out to you accurately and scientifically how you are to proceed to get what you want. And when it has spoken swing into action immediately. Then as you move all obstacles will dissolve into thin air.

Adopt This Tap System

The idea is to keep the picture or pictures before you constantly. As an aid in the visualization of the things you want and to keep them uppermost in your thoughts, write a word picture of them on several small cards. (Business card size is convenient.) Keep them always in your possession and look at them as frequently as possible—bearing in mind the more often you glance at them and visualize the pictures the firmer become the impressions upon your consciousness. As a suggestion, pin one card above the mirror to be looked at in the morning when you shave. Permit the details of your wishes outlined on the card to increase as you continue to develop the mental pictures. Have another card convenient to look at while you eat your lunch—your dinner. Use the cards again just before you go to sleep. Keep it up. Tap, tap, tap. However, there's no point to writing down your wishes until you have determined that every single detail of what you want is to be photographed permanently in your thoughts—to stay there until they become realities.

Use Small Cards

Remember that repetition of the same thought, the same suggestion, makes the picture positive.

T. N. T.

When you thoroughly comprehend this you will understand why thought always correlates with its object. Reflect for a moment. Where did the steamboat, the locomotive, the automobile, the electric light, the sewing machine, the radio, the typewriter and a million more objects and conveniences come from? All were thoughts or mental pictures in the minds of men before they became realities. Everything on this earth, except that which nature creates or has provided, is the result of sustained thought.

Powerful Thoughts Attract

Thought, contacting "**THAT SOMETHING**," brings everything, with nature's exceptions, into manifestation. A single thought not to be followed up—a flash to be dismissed or lost—is like a bobbing cork, aimless and without purpose. However, the same thought, the picture of the thing you want kept constant, always attracts it object, just as a magnet attracts. The larger and more powerful the magnet, the greater its drawing force and so it is with sustained thought—the more powerful it becomes the more it attracts. Just as a huge magnifying glass drawing the sun's rays and kept focused on a certain spot will burn a hole so will powerful sustained thought (the vivid mental picture) directed to or on its object correlate. However you must mentally see the picture of your object or ideal as a reality—see every detail of the picture as being in existence just as you want the object or ideal to actually be—then as if by magic the chain will link itself together. Now go back and reread this again until it is permanently impressed upon you.

As an additional means of concentration augment the foregoing formula with the use of a mirror. Daily and as frequently as possible study yourself in the glass. Search deeply into your eyes until you can see the fire of enthusiasm mount and cold, steely determination take the place of doubt and indecision. Get to know yourself thoroughly and keep telling yourself where you are going and what you want. Sooner or later you will see, mentally, at least, the reflection of your inner most desires in the mirror and your day dreams will begin to take shape. (As you grasp the science behind this theme you will understand why many powerful characters have used this mirror idea with great effectiveness.) Once the pictures are clearly defined do not for an instant

Use Your Mirror

T. N. T.

permit them to escape. Hold them with bands of steel.

> *"So use all that is called Fortune. Most men gamble with her, and gain all, and lose all, as her wheels roll. But do thou leave as unlawful these winnings and deal with Cause and Effect, the chancellor of God. In the Will work and acquire, and thou hast chained the wheels of Chance, and shall sit hereafter out of fear of her rotations."*
> EMERSON'S SELF RELIANCE.

Constant practice of writing down your wishes and using a mirror will work wonders. Shortly you can form the pictures at will—without the use of either cards or mirrors—and you will find yourself tapping the subconscious mind almost automatically. Practice, practice—always keep tapping.

Don't be afraid of over-doing, or becoming extravagant with your wishes and desires because, as I said before, you can have every single thing you wish, but you must become adept at doing exactly as I tell you.

Start Wishing and Doing

When you visualize and keep the pictures constant, action follows because action after all is nothing more than energized thought. Never lose your vision (your mental pictures)—for it is as King Solomon said nearly 3000 years ago:

"*Where there is no vision, the people perish.*"

Bear in mind this whole theme is as old as man. The only thing I do is to give you the message in words of today and outline a simple system of mechanics which may be used by anyone.

As we all know, "*the proof of the pudding is in the eating,*" and it you have any doubts as to whether or not I am giving you an exact science, try it. The automobile will begin to take shape, you will get the new shoes and the bricks of the mansion will fall into place as though a magical hand has touched them.

I know it, I believe it and it's so.

You know something of the efficacy of prayer. What is prayer but the expression of a heartfelt, earnest, sincere want or desire? The Great Master said:

"*What things soever ye desire, when ye pray BELIEVE that ye receive them, and ye shall have them.*"

T. N. T.

And it's true. All of us know the effect of our own desires on ourselves and how events are influenced by great desires. Every economic change down through the centuries has been due to the desire of man to benefit himself. However, we must **BELIEVE**—have **FAITH**—otherwise our innermost desires (prayers) become simply bursting bubbles.

The Great Master also said:

> *"If thou canst **BELIEVE**, all things are possible to him that **BELIEVETH**."*

I have pointed out the way that **BELIEF—FAITH** is engendered and kept constant — through repetition, reiteration of the same thought. It's now up to you to do the rest. Keep in mind always, as I said before you are appealing to the subconscious—"**THAT SOMETHING**" way down deep in all of us—universal thought—to the powerful force behind—that omnipotent power—a supreme intelligence—or whatever you wish to call it.

It is easier to go with the current than fight against it, but you must harmonize with others, with everything around you.

The Ancients Tapped

> "No longer let thy breathing only act in concert with the air which surrounds thee, but let thy intelligence also now be in harmony with the intelligence which embraces all things."
>
> THE WORDS OF A GREAT PHILOSOPHER.

It shouldn't be necessary for me to explain that I am suggesting that you put yourself in tune with the very stream of life itself. You who understand will appreciate that nature provides ways and means for all things to grow rightly. Meditate for a moment and you'll realize I am giving truths which many may have forgotten. **There's the great fundamental law of compensation which makes all things right.**

There's no set rule for doing anything because some of us perform one way and some another, just as two people go across the river—one goes by one bridge and one another—but they both ultimately get to their destination. In other words, after all is said and done, it's results that count, and, if you will make up your mind to exactly what you want and follow the simple rules which are given herein, everything you are after will be yours.

T. N. T.

I know it, I believe it and it's so.

After you get a grip on the **POWER** do not let the results of its usage surprise you.

Miracles will be performed.

You will do what previously you thought impossible.

As certain as night follows day, results will follow in a most astounding manner. Things will come to you from the most unexpected sources. Ideas for accomplishment will pop here and they'll pop there—then follow through. Others may say that as things happen for you, they are mere coincidences, that you are lucky, etc. Care not what they say. They are the scoffers, the non-believers, the ignorant. Remain steadfast in your **BELIEF** that they are the result of your own works coupled with "**THAT SOMETHING.**"

Tell No One

In using this **POWER** you are setting up powerful vibrations among the unseen forces, therefore it is not well that you should tell anyone—not even your most intimate friends or relatives—of your inner most wishes or desires—your deep rooted ambitions. Keep them to yourself, for should some person learn what you are after they may, consciously or unconsciously, due to enviousness, or something else, set up counter vibrations, place obstacles in your way and otherwise attempt to hinder you. Should barriers accidentally fall or be placed in your path, climb over or go around them. Go whistling blithely by.

Now remember it is entirely up to you as to the kind of pictures you create and hold constant and subsequently bring into realities. Analyze this: **YOU** are today exactly where your thoughts have brought you and you will be tomorrow where your thoughts take you. **YOU** are the absolute boss. Therefore, bear in mind always, the only limit is the limit you fix for yourself and remember you start with your thoughts. It may take longer to get some of the things you are after than others. But never get discouraged Rome was not built in a day. Just maintain your **FAITH**—your **BELIEF**—and keep tapping away. Many things will be added unto you and your dreams (the positive pictures) will come true.

Remember nothing can stop you but yourself.

I know it, I believe it and it's so.

I also am one of those who believes that all things

T. N. T.

are relative. To my way of thinking if a man can earn one dollar he can as easily earn ten. If he has two suits of clothes—he can have ten. The only difference is the amount of energy he is willing to expend and this goes for acquiring $100 to $1000 and from then on it is a matter of only adding ciphers. There is no limit as to what a person may do or secure provided he makes up his mind and steadfastly and determinedly moves towards his goal.

> "*Look within. Within is the fountain of good, and it will ever bubble up, if thou wilt ever dig.*"
>
> AN ANCIENT SAYING.

As I said under Detonating Caps be careful how you use the **POWER** which is to be yours. It will act as a boomerang and destroy you and everything you hold dear if you use it for evil. Therefore, only use it for doing you and others the most **Good** and bringing **Happiness** for yourself and those around you.

Use It Only For Good

Do not talk or boast about what you may have done for others or of your good deeds. They will speak for themselves. Just continue to give thanks for the fact that you are on your way—that's enough.

— *Tap* — *Tap* — *Tap* —

Have You Got "It?"

What is personality? What is it, when you get in the presence of another person who has personality, that grips you? What is it that causes you to feel his very presence—that overshadows you? It's nothing more than a dynamic force coupled with will power which is drawing from that huge reservoir of the subconscious. There are millions of people who have this personality—some say it's natural with them—perhaps it is — but they are unconsciously using this **POWER**. In other words, it's sort of been thrust upon them and when that thing called personality is backed up with will power, things move.

To my way of thinking selling bonds, books, clothes, insurance, electric service, washing machines, is no different than selling any other commodity—selling yourself or selling ideas. I have found that trying to put over an idea, firstly I have had to believe in the idea—dream it, eat

T. N. T.

with it, sleep with it—I had to have it with me every minute of the day until it became part of me—the old idea of repetition again—and I know it works in selling commodities. You have got to know what you are talking about and only hard, personal, persistent, intelligent study will enable you to do this.

One more thing, and that is keep informed as to what is going on in the world about you. You never know what a prospect may be interested in and it's sometimes necessary to get his attention or your "*break*" entirely through irrelevant subjects—that's why I repeat, read the newspapers, current periodicals, and read them thoroughly. I don't mean read every detail of some murder or suicide, but get a digest of the day's news.

Awaken, know what is going on about you. Get understanding.

Tap No. 3
Keep step with the world's affairs. The better informed a person, the better he is equipped to get what he wants.

Don't forget that Knowledge is Power—all of you should know that by this time.

"He who knows others is clever, but he who knows himself is enlightened."
    FROM THE SAYINGS OF A WISE ORIENTAL.

Increase your knowledge and the scope of your activities will be enlarged and the desire for greater things—larger things, will come automatically and, as they do, the things which you previously thought you wanted will become to your mind trivial and will be disregarded, which is another way of saying that you ultimately will hitch your wagon to a star and, when you do, you'll move with lightning-like speed.

Study, learn and work. Develop a keenness of observation. Step on the gas. Become alive for yourself and you'll pass it on to the other fellow. Get confidence, enthusiasm and you'll set up like vibrations all around you and that's the theory of all life—as old as the world itself. Like begets like—a laugh brings a laugh—a good deed calls for a good deed—riches beget riches, love, love—and so on.

The old law of attraction stated in Ampere's theory of electrical magnetism is: *"Parallel currents in the same direction attract one another"*—and when you are out of tune and antagonistic

T. N. T.

you put others out of tune and make them antagonistic because: "*Parallel currents in opposite directions repel one another.*"

However, don't get the thought that I have given you an over-size wishbone which will enable you to sit down and, by talking to yourself, through the idea of repetition, get what you want, because it will never work. You have got to have the wishbone backed up with a backbone and that isn't all—the wishbone and the backbone must be coordinated and synchronized to a point where they are running in perfect harmony, and when they are in tune, you will find personality developing. Then put action, energy into your scheme and everything will move before you.

Wishbones Need Backbones

I take it that all of us have admired that intense type of person. I mean by that, one whose shoulders are back, whose chest is out, whose head is up and whose eyes are alert. It is easy to pick out in any organization those whose feet lag, whose shoulders droop, whose chins sag and whose eyes are a blank. Drifters, loafers, quitters. First measure yourself. Then study those with whom you are associated and you can tell at almost a glance those who will make progress and those doomed to failure.

Every physical movement tells a story—each marks your personality. Your body and your mind are in reciprocal relationship—each acts and reacts upon the other. Your bodily movements—your facial expressions indicate the way you think. Now study yourself—your eyes—in the mirror again. The person you see in the mirror is the one the other person sees. What kind of an impression do you wish to make on him? That, too, is up to you. You know whether or not you have personality. If absent or undeveloped make up your mind to get it—you can and you will when you make up your mind, and do as suggested herein.

The Eyes Have "It"

If you will develop that intensity of purpose, determination to get ahead, shortly that determination will show in your eyes. You have heard people say that a certain person has a penetrating gaze—that he looks right through one. What is it? Nothing more than that fire from within—intensity—or whatever you wish to call it, which means that the person who has that gaze usually gets what he wants. Remember the eyes are the

T.N.T.

T. N. T.

windows of the soul. Look at the photographs of successful men—study their eyes and you will find that every one of them has that intensity; therefore, I say, let it be reflected in the way you walk, in the way you carry yourself and it will not be long before people will feel your presence when you walk through a crowd—and an individual prospect will feel that personality when you talk with him.

All of this is to explain that it takes an affirmative type to make progress and the things I have pointed out may be utilized to develop you into an affirmative type. The negative type is sunk before he starts. Nature takes care of these situations through the old law of the survival of the fittest. We know what happened in the day of Sparta when children were put on their own at a baby age and only those who survived were given further chance. A negative type is a quitter, or, another way, a quitter is a negative type and, while there is no point to going around hitting everybody on the nose just to start something, always remember it's poor business to let yourself be put on the defensive as that is a negative sign. The person who won't be licked, can't be licked. If you are taken unawares and suddenly put on the defensive, snap out of it. Take the offensive because, if you remain on the defensive, you are beaten.

Of course, to bring about this intensity of being, it's necessary to be in good health. I do not claim that the power of will is a cure-all to mend broken legs and all that sort of thing, but I do know that constant application of the theory herein advanced will aid a person in ill health. All of you have heard of Dr. Emil Coue, the Frenchman, who was in this country a few years ago, telling people they could cure themselves if they would adopt his plan. His idea was that you should say to yourself—*"Every day, in every way, I am getting better and better."* Just ponder over that for a minute.

Every Day— in Every Way

There was nothing new in that idea, any more than there is in the ideas which I put forth. Simply another way of expressing the whole scheme—reiteration, repetition—keeping upper most in your mind all the time what you want and which positive thoughts, in turn, are passed on to the subconscious mind—the wonder thing. **Think health, wealth and happiness and they will**

T. N. T.

all be yours. It cannot be otherwise.

We all know of people who are continually talking about backaches, headaches or some other kind of aches. They harp on them and the first thing they know, with that reiteration, the aches become realities. If you have such an ache or pain there is no point to talking about it; neither is there any point to talking about your worries, your troubles. Do not talk about them. Do not think about them. Then they will not be in your mind. It is the repetition that keeps them there. Shift your gears—reverse the process. Get away from the negative side and become an affirmative type—think affirmatively and the first thing you know your aches, worries and troubles will disappear.

> *"If thou art pained by any external thing, it is not this thing which disturbs thee, but thy own judgment about it. And it is in thy power to wipe out this judgment now. But if anything in thy own disposition gives thee pain, who hinders thee from correcting thy opinion?"*
> PHILOSOPHY OF THE AGES.

Are You in Reverse?
When a train roars across the track in front of you, you put on the brakes of your automobile, throw the gears into neutral and idle your engine—you are on your way again just as soon as the train passes but you certainly do not throw your gears into reverse and go backwards.

Compare yourself to the gears of your automobile. In reverse place all fears, worries, troubles, aches and pains. And when things go wrong simply put on the brakes, idle your engine until you can clearly see the road ahead. In high is everything you desire: health, wealth, happiness—success. No power in the world except your hand can put the gears of your automobile in reverse. If your own gears get in reverse remember you alone put them there. And you put them there with your own thoughts because:

> "There is nothing either good or bad, but thinking makes it so."
> HAMLET—*Act ii, Sc. 2.*

Therefore, as you think, you move either forward or backward—in high gear or in reverse. When you place yourself in reverse, worry, stew and fret you are using the tap, tap idea to bring into existence the things you would most avoid.

T. N. T.

Some 3500 years ago Job said:

> "*For the thing which I greatly feared is come upon me, and that which I was afraid of is come unto me.*"

Certainly they came upon him because he, in his fears pictured them—he used the immutable law to attract them. Just as you bring the good things which you want into reality by holding the positive thoughts constant so do you bring the bad things—those which you fear—by holding the worry, the negative thoughts constant.

If you have read this far then you must realize that when you look after your thoughts—then your thoughts will look after you. **Which Will It Be?** Therefore, which will it be—grief, trouble, ill health, worry, failure or health, wealth, happiness—success? It's entirely up to you—no power on this earth but you can direct your thoughts—and the way you use your **WILL** to keep your thoughts positive is a matter solely under your control. Therefore, lose no time in erecting a steel wall on the right side of the reverse gear, close the door of yesterday—keep it closed always—then shift from low gear into high and stay there.

Those of you with your own business, increase your business—or if you're a salesman, your sales —as a result of your own thinking. When others tell you that business is bad, things are tough, going to the bow-wows, etc., and you accept their thoughts and make them your own, your business will go to the bow-wows. Have no doubt about that. Then as you talk to others, with your chin on your chest, your feet dragging and the front of a professional mourner, then you tap them down and the more you circulate and the more you talk (tap, tap, tapping with the same story) especially, if you think and talk with an air of conviction, the more damage you do. You are setting up *"thought"*—in reality **FEAR**—vibrations which are far reaching. Fear thoughts are terrifically contagious and spread like wild fire. Conversely as you direct your thoughts (visualizing) towards increasing your business, your sales, your profits, etc., have no misgivings of your own (keeping your mind closed to the downward tapping thoughts of others) and put enthusiasm, energy and action into your program, your business, your sales automatically will increase. You must keep in mind always that the intense fire of enthusiasm from within

Close Your Ears

T. N. T.

becomes a conflagration which affects all on your wave length as long as you radiate it. The vibrations you set up with your powerful rays of enthusiasm inspire others, raise them up, build and attract business—just as **FEAR** vibrations tap others down, repel and destroy.

It is an indisputable fact, irrespective of the times, that there is always business somewhere for the man who **BELIEVES** it exists and goes after it but none for the person who is positive that none exists and makes no endeavor to move.

ACCEPT THIS!

EXPERIMENT, AND BE CONVINCED.

Any downward or upward trend in our world wide economic scheme is due entirely to the way we think. When the great world leaders —the statesmen, the financiers, editors, publishers, economists — those who direct and influence the thoughts of millions in every part of the globe permit depressed thoughts to enter into their scheme, then depressed thoughts and **FEAR** vibrations enter into the scheme of those same millions and business comes to a near standstill. When the

Thought Moves the World

world's leaders change their way of thinking—toss out **FEAR** and move forward instead of backwards, then the thoughts of millions change for the better and as they think constructively business improves.

Stop and meditate over this for a few moments. You will realize that *"thought"* operating in reverse was the great underlying factor which brought on the so-called economic depression. Human beings are human beings the world over —whether in Prague or Timbuctoo—all subject to the same emotions, the same influences, the same vibrations; and what is a community, a city, a nation but merely a collection of individual humans?

"As a man thinketh in his heart—so is he."

As members of a community think—so they are; as a city thinks—so is it, and as a nation thinks—so is it.

There is no other conclusion.

"We are living in a great crisis in human history. There is unlimited need for boldness and courage, but there is no occasion for dis-

T. N. T.

may. On the one hand there is the way to such achievements, to such wealth and happiness as mankind has never before known . . . life, even as we know it now, tastes very good at times. We spoil it a lot for ourselves and each other by fear, follies, hate, bickering, suspicion and anger. There is no need for us to go on spoiling it. We have not the health we might have. We have not a tithe of the happiness we might have. But it is within the power of the human will to change all that."
   H. G. WELLS
      ENGLAND'S GREAT MAN OF LETTERS.

— Tap — Tap — Tap —

This power—this vital energy—or whatever it is, is inexhaustible, and it is so easy to use it if you only have the key. I am fully appreciative of the fact that psychologists maintain that few persons really think.

Change Gears Now

It is my hope that this message will cause **You to Think.** If you dismiss it as so much balderdash, then I shall know that you have never understood or appreciated how the great characters of history whom I have previously mentioned and many others with whom you yourself should be familiar made names for themselves or gained niches in the hall of fame.

Real people—successful people, are those who made themselves and not what others made them. After all, there are only two ways to move, forward and backward—why not forward? Watch the down-and-outer on the street. His whole trouble is lack of positive ideas. If he thinks he is down and out—he is. If he will change his ideas, he will be up and coming. All of us know that.

You can shift your gears if you only realize it. You have been told how to keep out of reverse and it is simply a mechanical process for yourself. Understand and you will always keep your gears in high and move forward.

— Tap — Tap — Tap —

Believe in Your Goods
A sale is effected by getting a prospect to think as you do and, unless you believe that the thing you are selling is good then, obviously, you can't make the other fellow believe it.

That is just plain common sense—so, for those of you who may be selling keep in mind what I have

T. N. T.

previously said about knowing your article and selling yourself—that is 99% of the success of selling—the other 1% is leg work contacting the prospect.

You should realize that the bending other people to your will or getting them to do as you wish is simply having them think as you think and that is very easy.

Charles M. Schwab said: "*Many of us think of salesmen as people traveling around with sample kits. Instead, we are all salesmen, every day of our lives. We are selling our ideas, our plans, our energies, our enthusiasm to those with whom we come in contact.*" So it is with every endeavor, and especially true of selling commodities because you must contact people.

Sell Yourself

And when I say contact, I mean contacting them face to face. The day of order taking is gone and it is only the persons who have got it in them who are to succeed now—all the others will sink. You cannot beat a fundamental law—"*the survival of the fittest.*" Therefore, forget about order taking and keep in mind the only way you can close a sale is to make the prospect think as you think — the best way is in face to face contact—you have got to be in his presence—you have got to see his reactions—"*the old law of cause and effect*"—and you have got to adapt yourself to the conditions as they confront you with that individual prospect.

If you are intent on making a sale—and you must be if you are going to succeed—keep in mind my **Follow Your Hunches** theme. The subconscious mind will be giving you ideas, hunches, inspirations, a perfect flood of them, which will guide you correctly. They will point out the way to get into a busy man's presence—into the privacy of his very self and, when you get there, stand on both feet.

Be alert. Make him feel your personality. Know what you are talking about. Be enthusiastic. Don't quail.

You are just as good as he is and, besides, you may have something which he hasn't and that is utmost confidence, utmost faith in the article you are selling. On the other hand, if he is a success he also has personality—therefore, be sure to put the contact on a fifty-fifty basis. Do not belittle him—do not let him belittle you. Meet on common ground. Make him like you and when

T. N. T.

he likes you and you him, success is on its way. Remember you are going to sell him.

There is strength in team work. The esprit de corps pounded into those of us who were in the army made the American forces what they were—and it's the esprit de corps, team work, determination to move forward which will shove us along. If this is accepted in the spirit in which it is given; put into execution, you will be unbeatable. And by getting in tune and getting others on the track, the world is yours.

> *"When Fear rules the will, nothing can be done, but when a man casts Fear out of his mind the world becomes his oyster.*
> *To lose a bit of money is nothing, but to lose hope—to lose nerve and ambition—that is what makes men cripples."*
> HERBERT N. CASSON.

Ascertain exactly what you want and use the mechanics given and you will discover more gates open for you than you ever dreamed existed. I am not interested in any prophetic explanations—I am interested in results. A light will dawn upon you and you will see clearly ahead how to achieve what you are after. The same principles, the same methods can be successfully applied to any line.

The ability to accomplish anything in a convincing fashion depends entirely upon the degree of expert knowledge which you possess coupled with that intensity of purpose. Read and study, practice, practice, tap, tap, tap.

Before closing I should tell you that the conscious mind must be placed in a receptive condition to get the ideas from the subjective or subconscious. Of course, we all know it is the conscious mind which reasons, which weighs, which calculates—the subconscious mind does not do any of these things—it simply passes on ideas to the conscious mind.

Open the Door

You have heard a lot of people say: *"play your hunches"*—what are those hunches? Where do they come from? They come from the workings of the subconscious mind. Psychologists tell us—you will soon understand the reason—that to put the human mind in a receptive condition you must relax. If you have ever laid on the massage table and been told by the masseur to relax then you know what I mean. Let the body go limp. If you have trouble at first, try it with your arm—both arms —both legs, until the whole body is relaxed and the mind automatically will relax. When that

Relax and Tap

T. N. T.

is accomplished concentrate on what you want—then hunches come. Grab them, execute them as the little voice tells you. Do not reason or argue, but do as you are told and do it immediately.

You will understand what psychologists, mystics and students mean when they tell you to stop, relax—**Think of nothing**—when you wish to draw on the subconscious and have the little inner voice speak. As you further progress you will also begin to realize what the seers of the East had in mind when they said: *"Become at ease, meditate, go into the great silence, continue to meditate and your problems will fade into nothingness."*

The road ahead will become illuminated and your burdens will fall away one by one. Is there anything clearer than *"Pilgrim's Progress"*? My message is no different than that which was conveyed there—only, as I said before—I put it to you in perhaps different words.

The late Thomas A. Edison explaining his success of inventing said: *"I begin by using my accumulated knowledge but most of my inventions are completed with **Ideas** which flash into my mind out of thin air."* Fred Ott and Charles Dally, associ-

The Mysterious Nothingness

ated with Mr. Edison for more than 50 years, solved the secret of making synthetic rubber.

I quote from a newspaper story dated October 21, 1931: *"On Monday, he (Mr. Edison), started to sink into a stupor. But Dally and Ott were still pounding doggedly (determinedly, concentrating, tap, tap, tap) at their experiments. And on Tuesday night the solution flashed out of the mysterious nothingness."*

The little voice spoke—just like it always does when you make up your mind what you want and when you go after it.

If your own little inner voice suggests that you ask for something, do not be backward about asking. You have nothing to fear. The other person will never help unless he knows your wishes so you must ask.

Accept the theory advanced herein and practice intelligently and the voice will speak just like it did for Edison, Ott, Dally and thousands of others, and you will get results—all will be yours.

In Julius Caesar, Cassius, he of the lean and hungry look, talking to Brutus, of the Roman Em-

T.N.T.

peror's power, said:
> "*The fault, dear Brutus, is not in our stars,*
> *But in Ourselves that we are underlings.*"

As you know, William Shakespeare wrote that, and he himself arose above the commonplace by using this **POWER**.

If you are timid, backward, in a rut and an underling, it is because of yourself. Blame not the stars. Blame not society. Blame not the world. Blame **Yourself**. Again I say, change gears. Put them in **High** and **Begin to Move**.

Who Is to Blame?

Some people not thoroughly understanding may say that you are conceited, self-centered, or selfish but care not what they say. Those are the scoffers—those who would put rocks in your road and otherwise impede your progress. Those who understand will be helpful—they will be eager to serve you. The intelligent ones will begin to study you to determine what you have that they haven't and try to learn your secret.

Grip Tightly

I have given you a grip on it; hold it to you tightly and start moving forward.

George Jean Nathan, one of America's foremost critics, in a compilation of "*Living Philosophies*" declares he has never known a man who succeeded in life in a material way who did not think of himself first, last and all the time. Naturally I don't know just how Nathan meant that but I am sure he did not mean that a successful man is selfish to the point where he isn't helpful to others because if you follow the theme as I have outlined it and get on the road to success you will not be led to act ruthlessly.

As a matter of fact, the exact opposite is true because you will find that you will wish to do charitable things, good things for other people, performing services involving the throwing out of crumbs as it were, and your willingness to do something for the other fellow will bring about a willingness on his part to do something for you. There is nothing selfish about this—it's just a matter of cause and effect. Remember Ampere's laws of attraction. *Like begets like.* When you perform a service you will be paid huge dividends. There is no mystery about it, it's just so.

Service Pays Dividends

— *Tap* — *Tap* — *Tap* —

T. N. T.

"*I am the master of my fate,*
I am the captain of my soul."
HENLEY.

— Tap — Tap — Tap —

As a man thinketh in his heart—so is he.

— Tap — Tap — Tap —

I know it, I believe it and it's so.

— Tap — Tap — Tap —

T.N.T.—It rocks the earth!

This little book will do everything for you that is claimed but you must reread it and reread it until every sentence, every word is thoroughly understood and then you must apply the principles and mechanics with your whole heart and soul. Make them a part of your daily life and when you put into practice the ideas offered you will find that they will work just as they've always worked and always will. If you are in deadly earnest with yourself you will find the whole scheme very simple.

Practice Tap, Tap, Tap

After you have studied the book and have reflected upon the ideas set forth you will appreciate the tremendous force which lies in the science of thought repetition and positive action. You can, by repetition of the same thought, "tap" yourself upward or downward—dependent on whether you have depressed or constructive thoughts and as you build yourself **Reread It** powerfully you will find that you can **Reread It** influence others by your thoughts. **Reread It** Therefore, let me again admonish you to exercise great care that you do not misuse your **POWER**. Keep your mind filled with good, constructive thoughts and then act with all the energy you possess as the ideas come to you. Remember: *Every thought, kept ever constant, leads to action and results follow.* So keep this book and reread it, study it and reread and study it as frequently as possible. Practice, tap, tap, tap.

> *In the beginning all things were good. Man, himself, made them bad. You do evil and evil will be done you. You do good and you will receive good in return. You can be what you wish and have everything you want, provided, you are willing to pay the price in time, thought, effort and energy. You now have the key—may you make it work.*

T.N.T.—IT ROCKS THE EARTH!

T. N. T.

The theme of this book was broadcast daily for a month to many thousands by the author over K. G. W. (*well known Pacific Coast radio station—affiliated N. B. C.*). Excerpts have been read and the book referred to over the air frequently by many speakers.

READ THIS DIGEST COMMENT OF THOUSANDS

"Your series of "T.N.T." broadcasts are still coming back to this station. While you were on the air, I, personally, received calls every day from housewives and business men. Their general comment hinged on the fact that you had hit an optomistic note which could be practically applied. I write this letter because it takes more than the old sunshine in your voice to convince a hardboiled listening public that you know what you are talking about."

THE OREGONIAN—K.G.W. *by* CLIFF R. ENGLE

"The more you spread your message the greater will become the service you are rendering to your fellow men."
PAUL R. KELTY, *Editor*, THE OREGONIAN,
Portland, Oregon.

Many others believing that great good must follow, urged me to get my message circulated and this little book is the result. The whole theme came to be when I *"thought"* I was licked and knew not which way to turn. However, I was seeking and when *"ye seek, ye shall find."*

This book is published with the sincere desire that it will help everyone. Already it has helped thousands and it will help you. When you catch the "secret" of the book, tell others about it, for then you, too, will be rendering a service to your fellow men and it will pay you dividends. You, perhaps, have friends and acquaintances who are depressed; are in ill health; are worried over financial affairs; whose worlds are topsy-turvy; dissatisfied with their lot in life—lost in the wilderness. You may have a son or a daughter, a relative or know a boy or girl whom you would like to see make a place in the world. Place copies of this book into the hands of those you wish to help and admonish them to study it—rereading it as frequently as possible. Should you be unable to get copies from your local book dealer or the distributor from whom this copy came, write direct to the publishers.— *C.M.B.*

NOTE—Single copies One Dollar. Special discounts when purchased in quantities. We shall be glad to quote prices and answer inquiries.—T.N.T.—*Distributors*, 3204 East Burnside St.
Portland, Oregon

ALL WHO USE IT----PROFIT!!

Excerpts from a few of the letters from firms where executives and employes have copies:

OLDS, WORTMAN & KING (One of the oldest department stores on the Pacific Coast) bought 400 copies. D. D. JOHNSON, *General Superintendent*, wrote:—"Inasmuch as our executives, buyers and department heads are enthused over results from usage of 'T.N.T.—It Rocks the Earth', we are purchasing 400 more copies for distribution among our employes. Positive the book will do as claimed. If adopted generally there will be an immediate improvement in all lines of business."

INDEPENDENCE FUND OF NORTH AMERICA, INC., One Cedar Street, New York City, purchased 100 copies for salesmen. DOUGLAS LAIRD, vice-president, wrote:—"Ship us immediately 100 copies. It will have a great effect on anyone who reads it carefully and keeps following the thoughts contained in it."

SAM'L G. SUPPLEE & CO., 17-19 Union Square, New York City, bought 12 copies. MR. SUPPLEE wrote:—"It is a pleasure to review the book from time to time and I expect to make good use of it through our executive force."

ARTHUR L. FIELDS, *Chairman of the Board of Directors*, PORTLAND CHAMBER OF COMMERCE, 1933 and head of FIELDS MOTOR CAR CO., bought 11 copies. He says:—"I purchased 10 additional copies the first week in March and our business has shown a marked upturn since. March, April and May of this year will show a favorable profit instead of a decided loss for the same period last year."

MATTHEW LAHTI of MATTHEW LAHTI & CO., Boston, Mass., bought 5 copies and followed it with an order for 7 more, writing:—"Very interesting. It is the connecting link between the intangible and the tangible."

FRANK L. HAMON, *Division Cable Manager*, POSTAL TELEGRAPH-CABLE CO., wrote:—"Bought 20 copies for employes of the Portland office. Our business has increased a large percentage since the theme was introduced. Will make any firm or set of individuals more successful."

L. D. KORK, *Portland Manager* LYBRAND, ROSS BROTHERS & MONTGOMERY, bought 50 copies. He said:—"The fact that I bought 50 copies for distribution in our organization indicates what I think of 'T.N.T.—It Rocks the Earth.' It will get results wherever used."

THE WASHINGTON STATE FARM BUREAU of the STATE FARM INSURANCE COMPANIES of Bloomington, Ill., bought 30 copies saying:— "You have our permission to state the number of books purchased by our organization. Your good little book is still being used by members of this organization to the mutual benefit of all concerned."

FRED. E. GULICK, D.M.D., *President of the* ITECO LABORATORIES, Portland, Ore., with a world wide sales organization, bought 45 copies. He wrote:—"I want 20 more copies. Words will not express the good the books already placed in my organization have done for my people and my business. Sales have increased steadily since we found the 'Secret' in 'T.N.T.'. Every sales organization, every business concern, in fact all firms should have copies for their executives and employes and when they understand what is in the book and use it, they will give you their everlasting thanks just as you have mine."

H. A. GREEN, *President of the* DOERNBECHER MANUFACTURING CO., the largest furniture factory under one roof in the world, said:—"A wonderful piece of work. It is making the rounds of our entire organization."

MEIER & FRANK CO. (largest department store in the West) requested its employes to read the book. VIVIAN P. COOLEY, *Manager*, book department, wrote:—"Consistently continues to be one of our best sellers. We continue to get orders from all parts of the country. You know, of course, that our many employes were asked to read the book and I believe those who have applied the principles have been helped tremendously."

THE FIRST NATIONAL BANK, Portland, Ore., bought 10 copies for its branch managers. C. C. COLT, senior vice-president wrote:—"After I read it several times I was impressed with the thought that it was a splendid thing for anyone to use. As a starter I have purchased 10 copies for managers of our various branches."

FRANKLIN T. GRIFFITH, *President of* THE PORTLAND ELECTRIC POWER CO., THE PORTLAND GENERAL ELECTRIC CO., wrote:— "I'm going to use 10 copies as trial seed. You have set forth the vital principles of success . . . *Faith In Oneself*."

THOMAS (TOMMY) LUKE, formerly *President* FLORISTS' TELEGRAPH DELIVERY ASSOCIATION:—"I have had my employes read every edition a number of times. It is just what the name implies. It is exactly "THAT SOMETHING" you and I need most in our problems of today and tomorrow."

RICHARD G. MONTGOMERY, *Assistant Manager*, THE J. K. GILL CO., (largest book dealers on the Pacific Coast) said:—"Just to let you know your book is still eagerly sought after. I do not know how many times we have repeated our orders for additional copies but I do know your book has headed the list of our best sellers since it was first published. Literally, it sells itself."

ZELL BROS., well known northwest Jewelers, bought copies for all major employes. J. S. ZELL wrote:—"Can't say too much for it. Biggest, little volume I've ever read. I have procured copies for all my major employes."

The late CHARLES F. BERG, after 20 copies were put to use in his organization, CHARLES F. BERG, INC., wrote:—"Wish everybody could have a copy. I especially recommend it to heads of firms where employes come in contact with the public."

WHAT OTHERS SAY.

WALTER P. CHRYSLER, *Chairman of Board and President of* CHRYSLER CORP.—"It is a very stimulating document and one that would be decidedly helpful to anyone who is interested in making his own place in the world."

MARIE DRESSLER, *Famous Screen and Stage Actress*—"What a book if used rightly!!" (She purchased 20 copies for friends).

GENE TUNNEY, 230 Park Avenue, New York City:—"It is a fine story, as old as man himself, told in a new way at a most opportune time. May I congratulate you."

ALFRED E. SMITH, *former Governor of the State of New York*—"Most interesting."

FRANK KNOX, *Publisher of* CHICAGO DAILY NEWS:—"Your booklet 'T.N.T.' makes interesting reading, contains many inspirational messages and should be most helpful."

THEODORE ROOSEVELT, *formerly Governor-General,* PHILIPPINE ISLANDS:—"I read 'T.N.T' with interest and liked it. It is full of good sound philosophy."

LEWIS E. LAWES, *Warden,* SING SING PRISON, author "20,000 Years in Sing Sing," wrote:—"It is of practical value to anyone who will follow its suggestions."

REV. S. PARKES CADMAN, D.D., *Pastor,* CENTRAL CONGREGATIONAL CHURCH, Brooklyn:—"I have read your booklet with keen interest ... I am glad that you are devoting your splendid energies in an effort to elucidate the problems which have hitherto challenged the best efforts of our finest thinkers."

JOHN E. EDGERTON, *Chairman of the Board, 1933,* NATIONAL ASSOCIATION OF MANUFACTURERS of the UNITED STATES of AMERICA.—"The most fundamental truths of life ... Possesses peculiar value. I both congratulate and commend you upon the excellent contribution which you have thus made to the *Most Essential Processes of Recovery* ... Almost envy you ... the great good which your work is accomplishing for others."

ROGER W. BABSON, *Economist and Statistician*—"I think it is fine. Keep up the good work."

EDWARD G. SEUBERT, *President,* STANDARD OIL CO., of Indiana:—"It is a dynamic presentation of the merits of a positive and confident approach to the problems of life."

COL. FREDERICK PALMER, *Noted War Correspondent*—"Have read your booklet, which was so dynamic that it emitted electric sparks as I turned the pages. It's a knockout."

RALPH BUDD, *President,* BURLINGTON LINES:—"I congratulate you on this work, and I believe the suggestions contained therein are very useful and helpful."

J. C. PENNEY, *Chairman of Board,* J. C. PENNEY COMPANY, INC.:—"I read it thoroughly and enjoyed it. I consider its philosophy so good that I am passing it around among my friends."

AMOS PARRISH, *of* AMOS PARRISH AND COMPANY, New York City:— "You are to be congratulated on a fine piece of work. We found it most interesting."

GEN. W. W. ATTERBURY, *President,* PENNSYLVANIA RAILROAD COMPANY:—"Most interesting and worth while."

JOHN B. KENNEDY, *Associate Editor,* COLLIER'S:—"I enjoyed reading the booklet, and believe it should have a great effect on the public."

WALTER A. STAUB, *Partner,* LYBRAND, ROSS BROS. & MONTGOMERY, New York City:—"I have read it with interest and am particularly impressed with its timeliness. If we could set off enough charges of your T.N.T. of faith, courage and determined 'tap, tap, tap,' it would break up the present jam of fear, pessimism and feeling of impotence. We certainly need it."

R. A. BAKER, *of* COLLEGE OF NEW YORK; *Secretary of* DIVISION OF CHEMICAL EDUCATION of the AMERICAN CHEMICAL SOCIETY:— "The point of view which you present in your booklet is a powerful one. I can readily see how it would enable many people to achieve an independence of thought and philosophy which would enable them to rise above their immediate difficulties."

CHARLES T. SIDLO, *of* SIDLO, SIMONS, DAY & CO., Denver, Colorado:— "Have read it through several times and am very much impressed with the message which it contains."

ALFRED J. DIESCHER, *Consulting Engineer,* Winfield, Kansas:—"Can aid anyone who reads it thoughtfully and observes its tenets faithfully."

M. E. TRAYLOR, *President,* AMERICAN TRUSTEE SHARE CORP., New York:—"I think you have a very interesting way of presenting a number of truths that cannot be brought to our attention too often. I am sure your book will be helpful to anyone who reads it in a receptive frame of mind."

REV. DANIEL A. POLING, *President,* CHRISTIAN HERALD ASSOCIATION, New York City:—"I like it immensely."

N. A. GLADDING, *Vice-President,* E. C. ATKINS & COMPANY, INC., Indianapolis, Ind.:—"Makes it a mighty valuable companion for one to carry around in his portfolio for frequent reference."

HENRY L. STEVENS, JR., *formerly National Commander,* AMERICAN LEGION:—"Am convinced of its worth-whileness and shall get out of it all there is in it for me."

EARL D. WISE, *Vice-President and General Manager,* THE PACIFIC TELEPHONE & TELEGRAPH COMPANY:—" 'T.N.T.—*It Rocks the Earth*' beats out all of its competitors for attention. I read it immediately and think it excellent. It pulls one along so irresistibly that there is no stopping in its reading. It registers from first paragraph to last."

CARL S. KELTY, LOS ANGELES EVENING HERALD-EXPRESS, Los Angeles, Cal.:—"You have caught from the ether something that has a mystical quality—a something that explains the magic of coincidence, the mystery of what makes some men 'lucky'."

MERLE THORPE, *Editor,* NATION'S BUSINESS:—"I agree with you that what we need today is to regain that elusive thing called confidence. Whatever can be done to bring this about is a public service at this time."

ORRA E. MONNETTE, *Vice-Chairman of Board,* BANK OF AMERICA, NATIONAL TRUST & SAVINGS ASSN., Los Angeles, Cal.:—"Should be helpful to individuals and organizations."

JOHN D. CURTIS, CURTIS, STEPHENSON & CO., Boston, Mass.—"Every one of normal intelligence has the desire to accomplish great things but does not force the stored ability locked up within himself to assert its full power. Your booklet surely is a master key to the lock and should inspire its readers to a realization of such desires."

PAUL R. KELTY, *Editor,* THE OREGONIAN, Portland, Ore.:—"Could the basic truth of your booklet but be fully apprehended and understood and held by all of us, life's problems would vanish into nothingness. Your presentation is very compelling. The more you spread it the greater will become the service you are rendering to your fellow men."

B. F. IRVINE, *Editor,* THE JOURNAL, Portland, Ore.:—" 'T.N.T.—*It Rocks the Earth*' carries a theme which will help all who will accept it. Mr. Bristol has a grip on 'THAT SOMETHING' which many seek but few find. I, too, know it, believe it and it's so."

B. P. GUILD, *Business Manager,* LOS ANGELES EXAMINER, Los Angeles, Cal.:—"Well worth while. You have put it over with a big punch. I defy anyone to read it without getting a real message. It is the truth and can be made to work out successfully in every day life."

E. C. SAMMONS, *Vice-President,* IRON FIREMAN MANUFACTURING COMPANY:—"It's a knockout. Your message is so forceful I am sure it will receive a great welcome everywhere."

TOM BURNS of Burnside, *Independent Thinker and Philosopher,* Portland, Ore.:—" 'T.N.T.' Touches the Spot because that reflex action of the nervous system called the mind can be pepped up by injections of the self confidence which is the essence of T.N.T. Besides sales people of the collapsed tissue type (and they are about nine out of ten) can be '*Born Again*' through the injections of T.N.T. which, when digested, is the *Ne Plus Ultra of Self-confidence.*'

CPSIA information can be obtained
at www.ICGtesting.com
Printed in the USA
BVHW040331060223
657936BV00002B/61